Growing up in
THE 1920s

Amanda Clarke

B.T. Batsford Ltd   London P8.95

Typeset by Tek-Art Ltd, Kent
and printed in Great Britain by
R J Acford
Chichester, Sussex
for the publishers
B.T. Batsford Ltd,
4 Fitzhardinge Street,
London W1H 0AH

ISBN 0 7134 5052 5

Frontispiece: **This photograph was taken while
the children were waiting for a go on the Big
Wheel at Blackpool.**

Acknowledgments

The Author and Publishers thank the following for
their kind permission to reproduce copyright
illustrations: Air Portraits, fig. 8; Beamish North of
England Open Air Museum, figs 65, 66; Rosemary
Booth, frontispiece and figs 13 (courtesy of Warwick
Antiques), 20, 21, 43 (courtesy of Mrs E. Wardle);
BBC Hulton Picture Library, figs 2, 5, 6, 9, 10, 23,
24, 31, 40, 41, 54, 68, 69, 70; Castle Museum, York,
fig 33; Mrs R. Clarke, fig. 37; Country Life
Publishers, fig. 12; Mary Evans Picture Library,
figs 4, 15, 67; A. Hart, figs 39, 44, 47; Lancashire
Library, figs 28, 29; Lancaster Library, fig. 27;
Marconi Ltd, fig. 7; Mrs V. Phillips, figs 53, 61;
Major and Mrs Purves, 45, 51, 52; Warwick County
Museum, figs 1, 14, 17, 18, 19, 25, 32, 34, 35, 36, 38,
42, 56, 60, 62, 63, 64; Warwick Record Office, figs 3,
11, 22, 26, 30, 48, 55, 57. Figs 16, 49, 50 and 59 are
from *Design in Modern Life* by John Goag,
published by Ernest Benn in 1925.

Contents

The Illustrations

1 The 1920s

Armistice was signed on 11 November 1918. With the end of the First World War, a new era of peace and prosperity was envisaged. Most people had high expectations of the 1920s and although the decade did not turn out to be as idyllic as they hoped, definite improvements were made in areas such as health, education and the standard of living.

It was a period of the "haves" and the "have-nots". The "haves" lived comfortably, ate well, dressed well and enjoyed a bright social life. The "have-nots" endured a very different state of affairs. Often the father of the family was out of work, the house was over-crowded and squalid, and food and clothes were in short supply.

Many mini-revolutions occurred in the Twenties, in the home, in dress, in travel, in the country, in communications and in attitudes towards women. For those who had money it was a decade of fun and excitement. For those who had not, it was far from pleasant.

The political situation

The political situation during the 1920s was extremely complex. In foreign affairs, it was soon discovered that all had not been solved by the First World War and that international differences were still numerous. Russia, with her threat of Bolshevism, was regarded with mistrust, and nearer home, Adolph Hitler in Germany and Benito Mussolini in Italy were growing in power. Attempts were made to prevent further disagreements by the Locarno Pact (1925) and the Kellogg Pact (1928). The former guaranteed the French frontiers and the latter invited all nations to renounce aggressive warfare. It had been signed by all major countries including the USA and the USSR by 1930.

At home, Ireland was a continual source of concern as more and more violent means were used by extremists to persuade the British Government to grant Ireland her independence. On the British mainland, unemployment and the worsening economic climate were the major issues to be dealt with, culminating in the crisis of the General Strike in 1926.

These problems would have been difficult for a stable government to cope with. However, during the decade there were six changes of government, and the emergence to power of a

1   A cartoon from 1927 of a "typical" Twenties' family out for a walk. Note the large perambulator, and the dummies firmly stuck in the mouths of the babies. The semis in the background are a good illustration of contemporary ribbon development.

new political party. For the last fifty years the Conservative and Liberal Parties had dominated the political scene, but by 1918 the Labour Party had emerged and was steadily growing in support and confidence. The first Labour Government was in power in 1924.

Many more people were entitled to vote in the 1920s than ever before. After the war there was universal male suffrage, and votes for women over the age of 30. An Act of 1928 allowed women over the age of 21 to vote also, a move which caused considerable concern at the time.

Industry, unemployment and strikes

The 1920s saw great advances in "new" industries such as cars, aircraft and mass-produced clothing. This was generally at the expense of "old" industries including shipbuilding, coalmining and weaving. In 1923, for example, 43.6% of shipbuilders, 21.6% of weavers and 3% of miners were unemployed. The worst-hit or "depressed" areas were the North, Scotland and Wales. In 1922 43% of the workers in Jarrow were out of a job, 49% in Barrow in Furness and 60% in Hartlepool. By the mid-Twenties over 2 million people were unemployed.

The Government refused to help as it considered that many workers were receiving too high wages, and that this, in turn, was putting up the prices of British-made goods. The slow but steady mechanization of many industries also meant that fewer workers were needed. Not many workers were prepared to accept lower wages or to lose their jobs and the result was a period of economic unrest. There were several strikes during the decade, the most significant being the General Strike in May 1926.

1929 saw the Wall Street Crash in America, and Britain was also engulfed by the world economic crisis which was to blight the next decade.

It has to be noted that while mass-produced goods and low prices were harmful to some industries, they also meant that many people could now afford things that had previously been considered luxuries and they were therefore able to enjoy a better standard of living.

The General Strike, 3-12 May 1926

Basically, the General Strike was over coalminers' pay. The Samuel Commission of April 1926 recommended that the miners receive a temporary reduction in pay or hours in return for such reforms as a family allowance. This did not go down well with the miners who took up the slogan "Not a penny off the pay, not a minute off the day!" The coal owners ignored their resentful feelings and proposed wage cuts.

Negotiations between the Government, the coal owners and the TUC (on behalf of the miners) began but broke down rapidly. On 1 May the Chairman of the TUC instructed the miners, railwaymen and transport workers to come out on strike. They were soon followed by the gas, electricity and building workers and by 3 May all unions affiliated to the TUC were out and the country had come to a virtual standstill.

2 During the General Strike in May 1926, many volunteers helped keep Britain going by driving trains, buses and trams, unloading goods at ports and mail at stations and acting as Special Constables. Here Mrs Talbot is driving a GWR (Great Western Railway) van which probably contained mail.

The Government declared a state of emergency and many people offered their services as volunteers, for example, to run transport, deliver mail and unload ships. At first, there was a carnival atmosphere, but the situation was becoming increasingly violent. Many trade union leaders were reluctant to

4 Terraces like these were numerous in the 1920s. There were no fields nearby for the children to play in and so the street was their playground. The girls in the foreground have a skipping rope, and there is a pram on the right-hand side.

pursue matters, and were frightened by the Attorney General's declaration on 8 May that the strike was illegal and that every striker could be sued. By 11 May the TUC was prepared to abandon the miners and re-open negotiations. On 12 May all but the miners returned to work and there was a thanksgiving service at Windsor attended by the King. The miners continued on strike, often in conditions of great personal hardship, until December, when they returned to work with the wage question unresolved.

3 These Council houses were built in a Warwickshire village during the early 1920s. The design is typical of the decade – semi-detached with three bedrooms, an inside lavatory and front and rear gardens.

Housing
In 1919 there was an acute housing shortage, with many families living in over-crowded, unsanitary conditions. Through Acts of Parliament of 1919, 1923, 1924 and 1930 the

7

Government promised to subsidize new houses built by local authorities. This led to the building of the first Council houses. Between 1919 and 1924 29,000 such homes were built, providing better accommodation for working-class families.

Many private houses, too, were built, and falling house prices and available mortgages meant that many families could now buy their own home. By 1930 over one million such "owner-occupier" houses had been built.

In spite of this extensive rebuilding and modernization, the Housing and Planning Committee of 1928 estimated that there were still in the UK one million houses that were unfit to live in, and two million that were grossly over-crowded.

"Bright Young Things"

With a life-style very different from "normal" during the 1920s, the "Bright Young Things"

5   A group of Bright Young Things enjoying one of the most important social events on their calendar – the Chelsea Arts Ball. Some are obviously in fancy dress and pierrots seem to be the most popular disguise.

scandalized many people by their madcap activities. They were a small group of upper-class young people who specialized in doing shocking things – drinking a lot, driving fast cars in a dangerous manner and indulging in outrageous behaviour. They loved playing pranks, especially at the expense of others. One young lady, at an important buffet party attended by many famous people, replaced all the ham in the sandwiches with pink flannel and then watched gleefully as the guests dealt with their surprise! Midnight bathing, treasure hunts and parties were also loved. At one party in 1928, all the guests arrived dressed up as babies. As the "Bright Young Things" were mostly titled people, all their antics were eagerly reported by the press, to the disgust of the more conservative members of society.

Women

During the war many women, by force of circumstances, had become more independent. Many had done "men's jobs" and when the war ended were not prepared to go back to their former, restricted way of life.

In the 1920s more women than ever before had a job and some achieved high positions, the most notable being Margaret Bondfield who in 1929 became the first woman Cabinet Minister. In 1928 women over the age of 21 were given the vote and this further enhanced their status. (The previous age limit had been 30.) For those who remained at home (and the vast majority did, once they were married), the situation was also improving. Families tended to be much smaller and homes were becoming much easier to run.

Their new-found freedom was reflected in fashion as women gaily abandoned their old corsets and long, heavy dresses in favour of short, loose frocks. Very "modern" girls also wore make-up, smoked in public and used slang.

Empire

As a revolt against the depressing economic

climate and to bolster morale, there was a patriotic revival. Empire Day (24 May, Queen Victoria's birthday) was celebrated annually and in 1924 Britain's glorious heritage was reinforced by the British Empire Exhibition at Wembley. This display covered 219 acres and every part of the Empire was represented. Attractions included a Wild West Rodeo, the Queen's Dolls' House, a statue of the Prince of Wales made out of butter, an Empire Pageant, a Military Tattoo which included a replica of the Battle of Balaclava, and an enormous amusement park. Catering was by J. Lyons. Although it was a huge financial loss, over 17

6 In June 1924 Queen Mary visited the British Empire Exhibition at Wembley. Here she is touring the African Village and being protected from the elements by an enormous African umbrella.

million people visited the Exhibition. The Wembley Stadium was part of this Exhibition and is all that survives today.

Entertainment

During the Twenties everyone was eager to enjoy themselves and there was a boom in popular entertainment. The radio, and the BBC, had the greatest influence. In 1922

◄ **7 Radio changed lives in the 1920s. This radio of 1922 is fairly sophisticated for, although it has a loudspeaker, no headphones are required. Notice the electric light.**

Sports were also considered important and the most popular included football, tennis, swimming, skating and greyhound racing.

Transport

Huge improvements were made in transport. Cars became available to anyone who could pay and by 1930 there were over one million private cars on the roads. In towns, trams and omnibuses provided a cheap and efficient service, while charabancs and motor buses opened up new possibilities for country people. No new railways were built, but the London Underground was extended to include the developing suburbs.

Aeroplanes were much loved. Flying exhibitions attracted large crowds and anyone who could afford it could buy his or her own aeroplane. A Gypsy Moth, for example, cost £595 in 1926. Passenger airlines became yearly more sophisticated and by the end of the decade were taking travellers to destinations all over the world.

Record breakers

The 1920s was a decade when many new records were set and there was a great sense of adventure and exploration. Many daring feats of endurance took place in the air, where new achievements were being made almost annually. In 1919 Alcock and Brown made the first transatlantic flight. In 1924 Sir Alan Cobham flew to India and back, and followed this the next year with a return trip to Cape Town. In 1926 he flew to Australia and back, taking a total of 230 flying hours. In 1927 Charles Lindbergh made his much-acclaimed solo transatlantic flight from New York to Paris. Women were not to be out-done, for in 1928 Amelia Earhart flew the Atlantic solo, and in 1930 Amy Johnson made her solo flight to Australia.

125,000 radio licences were issued; by 1930 the number had risen to 3,091,000. Television was also making an appearance although few families would have seen one. The cinema was enormously popular and Picture Palaces were built in almost every town. Gramophones and records improved in quality, and many people loved to dance.

New speed records were also set. In 1927 Major Henry Segrave beat the land speed record when he went over 200 mph at Daytona Beach in America. He was knighted in 1929 but was killed the following year in a speedboat on Lake Windermere.

There were also two unsuccessful attempts to climb Mount Everest, in 1921 and 1924; and in 1921 Sir Ernest Shackleton set sail on another expedition to the Antarctic. Swimming the Channel also appealed to some people and in 1926 Gertrude Ederle was the first woman to do so. She took a total of 14 hours and 39 minutes. On the cricket field J.B. Hobbs beat W.G. Grace's record by scoring over 126 centuries, in 1926.

8 This de Havilland DH51 was photographed in 1924. The picture gives a wonderful impression of the freedom and vulnerability of the pilot.

2 Homes

Over one and a half million new houses were built during the 1920s in an attempt to deal with the acute housing shortage. These new houses were generally either Council houses (built by local authorities with a government subsidy) or private houses. The new Council houses were usually built on large estates on the edges of towns. Rents varied between 10s and 13s (50-65p) per week.

Because of low house prices and the availability of mortgages, many families could now afford to buy their own home. This was a new idea, for previously most property had been rented from landlords. In 1920 a three-bedroomed semi cost £930; in 1930 the same sort of house cost only £397.

The new houses were often built on the edges of large towns (suburbs) or along main roads. (The latter was called ribbon

9 A comfortable drawing room in London, 1920. Notice the gas fire, ornate lampshades and the decorated border below the picture rail. There is a doll perched on the arm of the sofa.

development.) Most houses were built to a similar plan and contained a kitchen, scullery, living room and lavatory downstairs, and three bedrooms and possibly a bathroom upstairs. There was also a front garden for flowers and a back garden for vegetables. Twenties' houses were usually semi-detached, red-brick with slate roofs. They were sometimes livened up with mock Tudor beams, pebble dash and stained-glass windows.

Many old Victorian slums were pulled down during this period, and replaced by six-storeyed blocks of flats. These flats provided good accommodation with inside lavatories, running water, gas fires and communal laundries. Bungalows were also introduced in the early Twenties and became very popular. They were named after the Indian word "bunga" meaning mud dwelling and were

10 This is the interior of a working-class home in Bethnal Green, London. Although the date is 1924, the character of the room is very Victorian, with a cooking range, draped mantlepiece, wooden dresser and even an aspidistra. There is an air of prosperity which suggests that the father was in work. (Compare this with the other home in Bethnal Green on page 23.)

recognized as having only one storey. Many families, of course, lived in older houses, some in comfort but many in squalor.

Decoration

Modern homes in the 1920s veered away from the clutter and dark colours loved by the Victorians. Furnishings tended to be plain and simple. Walls were distempered in pale

13

◄ 11 **This advertisement of 1925 gives a good idea of how certain rooms were expected to be furnished and how much it cost to do so.**

colours and floral curtains and carpets (not fitted!) were popular. Furniture was generally made out of wood and often based on traditional period designs such as Elizabethan and Jacobean styles. By the end of the decade, however, tubular, metal-framed furniture was considered modern and chic.

The overall fashionable style of the 1920s (and of the 1930s) is known as Art Deco. This style was applied to everything, from dinner services to lights, from earrings to powder puffs! It tended to be bright and cheerful with a sense of fun. Today it is highly collectable and very expensive.

Heating and lighting

In the early Twenties most homes were lit by oil lamps, candles or gas lights, but by the mid-

12 **This comfortable nursery would have been affordable by wealthy parents. Notice the decorative frieze, the sturdy furniture, the fire guard, high chair at the table and pretty crib by the fire.**

13   Art Deco pottery often had a sense of fun. This charming trio are not just decorative but are, from left to right, an inkwell, vase and single flower holder.

Twenties electricity was becoming more popular. In 1926 the Central Electricity Board was formed. It developed the National Grid and made electricity available to more homes. By 1930 one fifth of all homes had electricity, but this was mainly in the towns.

The majority of families relied on open fires to heat their homes and their water, but gas or electric fires were being installed in most modern houses. In the winter children slept with stone hot-water bottles in their beds, for bedroom fires were lit only on special occasions.

The kitchen

Many women still coped with a Victorian kitchen, equipped with a cast-iron cooking range, a stone sink, a wooden dresser and a

14   This cover from a popular magazine of 1927 ►
gives a vivid insight into the housework of a modern young wife. In spite of having more freedom than ever before, women were still expected to be home-orientated.

copper for heating up water. However, a revolution was taking place and the emphasis was firmly on "labour-saving" devices.

Gas and electric cookers were becoming popular and, although ungainly by today's standards, they were far easier to use than a range. One of the first electric models to appear was the Baby Belling in 1919. This had two hot plates, a grill, oven and plate-warmer. In 1923 the first thermostatically controlled cooker came on the market and this introduced the regulo that we still use today.

In the same year, Frigidaire introduced their electric ice box – the forerunner of the modern fridge. It cost £60, the same price as a second-hand car.

527

ELECTRICAL DEPARTMENT
Labour-Saving Devices Which Save Both Time and Money

Please state Voltage when Ordering

E 69
MAGNET ELECTRIC OSCILLATING FAN
Bracket or Desk type
An exceptionally powerful type of Fan which can be adjusted according to requirements
£5 18 6

NEW MODEL
THE 'THOR' ELECTRIC WASHING MACHINE
An electric Washer and Wringer combined. Clothes can be thoroughly washed in the New 'Thor' Model in from 3 to 5 minutes, and the running costs are so low as to be almost negligible **£29 17 6**
Complete with Ironing Attachment **£39 17 6**

Complete booklet of Washing Machines forwarded on application

EL 5702 'MAGNET' COOKER
For a family of 4–6 persons. Cast iron door, door frames, hot table, etc., and with sheet steel body. There are 2 enclosed boiling plates, and a griller or toaster, spacious oven. Total loading 5,500 Watts. The oven and boiling plates are controlled by switches giving full, half and quarter heat. Price **£18 0 0**

Write for booklet showing full range of models

E 66
MAGNET ELECTRIC FAN
Desk or Bracket type, with current consumption of 34 watts
£4 6 6
State Voltage when Ordering

EL 555
'PROTOS' ELECTRIC FLOOR POLISHER
For cleaning and polishing Linoleum, Parquet Floors, and Painted Floors. 2 brushes covering 12 ins. of floor. Price complete with 23 ft cord, plug adapter, and 1 set of polishing brushes
£13 13 0
Other makes in stock

HOOVER
The Greater Hoover. Model 700 .. .. .. **£17 17 0**
A more popular priced Hoover Model (543) **£13 13 0**
Dusting tools for both models **£3 3 0**
Either may be had for **£1** down
Only the Hoover embodies the exclusive deep-cleaning principle of Positive Agitation. Hangings, carpet, upholstery, are cleaned easier, quicker and more thoroughly
Supplied with new Floor Polishing Attachment **£2 0 0** extra

EL 71 MAGNET ELECTRIC MASSAGE VIBRATOR
This is a valuable appliance, whether for medical use or simply as a toilet vibrator. The equipment includes six different types of applicators. Price.. .. .. **£4 15 0**

EL 28 MAGNET ELECTRIC WASHING MACHINE
Washing day without labour. Saves time and money. Washes 6 sheets or their equivalent in 15 minutes
£42 0 0
Attachments are available for the machine so that it can be used for making ice-cream, mincing and sausage making, knife cleaning, making butter, etc.

ALL PRICES ARE SUBJECT TO MARKET FLUCTUATIONS

In 1925 the American firm Hygena put the first kitchen cabinets on the market. These were eventually to replace the traditional dresser, and comprised of compartments, shelves and pull-out ironing board, work surface, flour sifter and egg rack.

All the new machines made life much easier for the housewife and kitchens tended to become smaller and more compact. Remember, however, that only a few mothers enjoyed such conditions. Most still had to work in kitchens that had no electricity or running water.

Electric equipment
During this period the market was flooded with a mass of household devices, some of them useful but some very silly. An electric iron could be bought for 18s (90p) but it weighed four pounds. Electric kettles were available but they took 12 minutes to boil. Other electric objects included teasmades, toasters, shavers and even mice-catchers! One doctor recommended that everyone should have a small electric shock a day to keep them in good health! Washing machines were also making a tentative appearance, but most mothers did a weekly wash involving a lot of hard work with a copper and mangle.

Bathrooms
At the start of the decade very few homes had a bathroom. Most children had a weekly bath in a hip-bath which was placed in front of the fire in the kitchen. Other families had fixed baths in the scullery. These baths often had a roll-top so that, when the bath was not in use, this made an additional working surface. Water for these baths had first to be heated up on the fire or in the copper, and several children would use the same water.

The Wheatley Housing Act of 1924 made it compulsory for any new house being built with a bath to have it fixed in a special bathroom. 1920s' baths were rather nice. They were usually free-standing and made out of cast iron and enamel. Water was heated by an overhead geyser.

16 This bathroom was designed by the well-known firm Twyfords in 1924. Only a few families would have been able to afford such an attractive bathroom.

3 Clothes

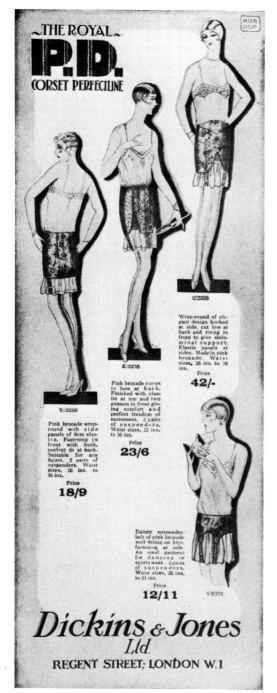

THE ROYAL
P.D.
CORSET PERFECTLINE

Wrap-round of elegant design hooked at side, cut low at back and rising in front to give abdominal support. Elastic panels at sides. Made in pink brocade. Waist sizes, 26 ins. to 36 ins.
Price
42/-

Z.5218
Pink brocade corset to lace at back. Finished with elastic at top and two gussets in front giving comfort and perfect freedom of movement. 2 pairs of suspenders. Waist sizes, 23 ins. to 36 ins.
Price
23/6

V.5250
Pink brocade wrap-round with side panels of firm elastic. Fastening in front with busk, perfect fit at back. Suitable for any figure. 2 pairs of suspenders. Waist sizes, 26 ins. to 36 ins.
Price
18/9

Dainty suspender-belt of pink brocade well fitting on hips, fastening at side. An ideal garment for dancing or sports wear. 2 pairs of suspenders. Waist sizes, 26 ins. to 33 ins.
Price
12/11   V.5275

Dickins & Jones
Ltd.
REGENT STREET; LONDON W.1

Clothing for both sexes underwent a revolution in the 1920s. Styles were produced that had never been seen before, and which frequently shocked the older generation. New clothes were lighter, brighter and far less cumbersome than ever before. Hair-styles also changed dramatically and, combined with the new clothes, gave the Twenties a distinctive look.

Women's clothes

Before the war, women had worn elaborate, full-length dresses with layers of restrictive undergarments. In the 1920s, body-crippling corsets were abandoned, hemlines rose and rose, and the boyish figure became all the rage. Dresses, or frocks as they were called, were low-waisted and by 1926 knee-length. They were often embroidered or decorated with beads and tassels. To complement the newly revealed legs, stockings became a daring flesh colour instead of the traditional black. Favourite accessories were dangling earrings and long necklaces. Fashionable colours mentioned in an advertisement for frocks and suits included "Roseda, Orchid, Bracken, Amethyst and Navy".

◄ **17** Although these 1920s' corsets look cumbersome to us, they were a vast improvement on the whalebone contraptions of a few years earlier. The corsets were light and designed to achieve the boyish figure.

18 A page from Weldon's catalogue, 1925. This ► was a popular magazine aimed at ordinary housewives. It included patterns so that you could make the clothes shown.

73057   73056

73060

73054

73055   73082

72488
Transfer No. 1341

M3445   73081

Bust sizes:
34, 36, 38, 40
and 44 inches.

PATTERNS
illustrated on this
page
6d. each, by post 7d.
Abroad 10d. each.

Bust sizes:
34, 36 and 38 inches
except where other-
wise stated.

Weldon's Transfers,
price 3d. each, by
post 3½d.

Weldon's Millinery
Patterns, 6d., by
post, 7d. Abroad,
10d. each.

Here are some typical prices, taken from newspaper advertisements in 1926: 59/9d (£3) for a frock, 89/9d (£4.50) for a two-piece (suit), 11/9d (60p) for a brassiere, 27/6d (£1.40) for an all-in-one corset and 14/11d (75p) for a pair of shoes.

The modern young woman, or "flapper" as she was sometimes called, was often bold enough to wear powder, rouge and pale blue eye-shadow in the evening, and may even have plucked her eyebrows. Some women were beginning to smoke, not only at home but in public, and this shocked many people.

Children's clothes

For the first time, children's clothes were designed with children in mind. Before the war, children had been dressed in similar styles to their parents. Again, these clothes were very restrictive and multi-layered and not much fun for playing in. Now girls wore simple cotton frocks, cardigans and canvas shoes in the summer, and serge skirts and hand-knitted jerseys in the winter. When it

19 Children's clothes shown in Weldon's summer catalogue, 1925.

20 This was a fashionable and popular winter creation for small children of either sex. The little girl is wearing a woollen coat, woollen leggings and a pull-on hat.

21 Menswear for every occasion, from Weldon's summer catalogue, 1927.

was cold, girls also wore liberty bodices, which were like long vests with suspenders attached, to keep up woollen stockings. Boys also had comfortable clothes. Knee-length trousers were worn in winter and summer. When it was cold, knee-length, turned-over socks and woollen jerseys were worn, whilst in the summer short-sleeved shirts and Fair Isle slipovers were popular. Boys generally wore short trousers, kept up with braces, until they were 15 or 16. Victorian lace-up boots were replaced with lace-up shoes for the winter and canvas shoes or sandals for summer.

Babies' clothes were made to be more comfortable and practical, too. No longer were babies dressed up in yards of lacy, white gown. By the end of the period romper suits, matinee jackets and short dresses were popular.

Men's clothing
Men's fashions also underwent a huge

transformation in the Twenties. Previously most men had worn formal three-piece suits. Now they were allowed far more casual styles as "cheerio" and "jazzy" fashions became acceptable. Flannel trousers, tweed jackets and brightly coloured Fair Isle slipovers were very popular, as were Plus Fours (baggy knicker-bockers) and Oxford Bags (trousers with very wide legs). In the summer, blazers and light-coloured trousers were complemented with a panama hat or a boater. By the late 1920s, pipe smoking and after-shave were desirable male accessories.

Hairstyles and hats

Before the war, women had been admired for the length of their hair. In the 1920s, almost every female, whether she was young or old, seemed to cut her hair – another sign of liberation and a completion of the Boyish Look. Short hair was known as a "bob". Variations included the "shingle", where the

hair was cut shorter at the back, and the Eton Crop, where the hair was given a virtual short-back-and-sides. Marcel Waves (perms) could curl hair, but for those who could not afford that, rags left in the hair overnight were the only alternative.

Men's hairstyles also changed and the short-back-and-sides became popular. (Previously men, too, had worn their hair longer.)

Hats were worn by everyone, including children. Women and girls wore head-hugging "Cloche" hats, often pulled way down over the ears and eyes. Boys wore caps, while men could choose from trilbys, Homburgs, Derbys, bowlers, panamas and boaters, to name a few.

22 This millinery advertisement appeared in a local paper in 1925. The hats are typical of the period. The top one was for day-time wear and the bottom one for evening.

4 Health

For many people the 1920s brought a considerable improvement in their standard of living, and this was reflected in their health. Low prices meant that better homes and better food were available to more families than ever before, and so people could enjoy greater comfort. Evidence supports this, for children were actually growing taller and people were living longer. By the late 1920s, the average life expectancy for men was 58.7 years, and 62.9 for women.

Although there was no National Health Service, the Ministry of Health had been set up in 1919. Its job was to look into housing conditions, cleanliness and the control of illnesses. Clinics were becoming more widespread and children received regular medical checks whilst at school.

In spite of the improvements, for a sizeable minority life was far from comfortable. For families on very low incomes all that was available was squalid, over-crowded rooms

23 This home in Bethnal Green contrasts sharply with that of the prosperous working-class family (page 13) living in the same area. Here the family is destitute and living conditions are horrifying. The family has only one room, one bed and a pram for the baby. There is a cooking range, but whether the family has any coal is debatable. Conditions like these were by no means rare.

and a poor, inadequate diet, which made them vulnerable to the greatest health risks.

Life on the dole

By the mid-1920s there were over 2 million people on the dole, and the number was rising steadily. The majority were men, many of whom were the sole breadwinners of their family. The maximum dole to which a man with a wife and three children was entitled from Social Security was 29/3d (£1.48) per week. The British Medical Association worked out that such a family needed at least 22/6½d (£1.13) per week for food to stay healthy, which would leave only a tiny proportion of the dole for rent, fuel and clothes. The result was that many people cut down on food or lived on unhealthy diets such as bread and margarine, and so many were badly under-nourished. Not only was their diet bad, but the only homes they could afford were those that had the lowest rent. These were usually Victorian slums with no running water, primitive cooking conditions and several people living and sleeping in one room.

Illnesses

Many children died every year from illnesses which today do not cause us concern, for there was no vaccination in the 1920s. Every year epidemics swept unchecked through schools and towns, with tragic results. The most feared illnesses were measles, diphtheria, whooping cough, scarlet fever, influenza and tuberculosis. In 1919/20, for example, an epidemic of influenza killed 15,000 in London alone. The discovery of penicillin in 1928 by Sir Alexander Fleming was the start of a dramatic improvement in treating certain illnesses.

Rickets was also a common illness, caused by vitamin deficiency. It affected many children and prevented their bones developing correctly.

If a child needed to go to hospital, his or her parents had to pay, something which families on the dole would have found almost impossible to do. The experience of being in hospital would have been far more frightening than it is nowadays. Often there were no special children's wards, and so a child would have found himself or herself in with adults.

24 The Ophthalmic (eye) ward in St Bartholomew's Hospital, London, in 1921. This looks a pleasant ward, but notice that it contains both children and adults. What method of heating is there?

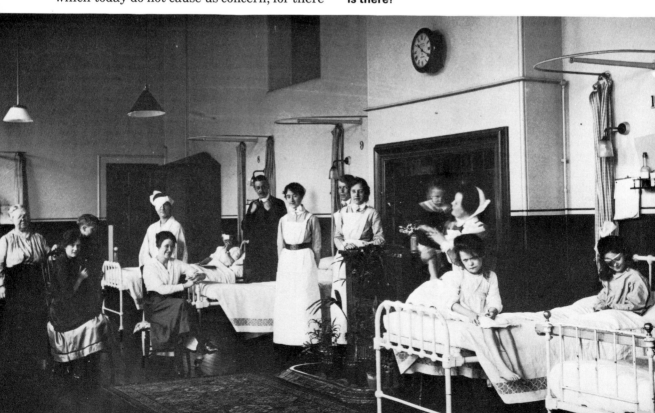

Parents were not allowed to stay or visit very regularly. In the more enlightened hospitals children's wards were decorated with tiled pictures depicting nursery rhymes, but the majority were bleak, frightening places.

Births

There was a fall in the birth rate during the 1920s. Two children per family became the average rather than four or five, as before the war. This again contributed to better standards of living, for there were fewer mouths to feed. In 1925, for example, in England and Wales, 711,000 babies were born, whereas in 1903 the number had been 948,000. The percentage of live births was higher and fewer children died in infancy.

Most women had their babies at home, attended by the local midwife, but wealthier mothers sometimes went into private nursing homes. Women were expected to stay in bed for at least three weeks after giving birth. Fathers were very rarely present at the births of their children. How does this compare with today's attitude?

Babies were usually christened within a few months of being born. Popular names included Nora, Edith, Muriel, Elizabeth (Betty), Margaret (Peggy), Joan, Marjorie and Mavis for girls, while boys might be called John, Eric, Donald, William (Bill), Harold, George, Percy, Ronald or Edward (Ted).

There was no Family Allowance.

Food and health

Families were becoming more aware of what they ate and the way it affected their health. New homes usually included a back garden where vegetables could be grown, and many people had allotments as well. More fresh fruit and vegetables were consumed, though tinned and bottled food was enjoying a boom. Packet mixes were also becoming more common and we would recognize many food items of the 1920s such as Bird's custard powder, Hartley's jams, Bournville cocoa and Oxo. The potato

crisp was invented by the French in the late 1920s and was an immediate success.

There was a move away from the traditional cooked breakfast to cereal. "Force", "Grapenuts" and porridge were popular, as were the "flake" types of cereals which became available by the mid-Twenties. The main meal was often eaten at midday, with a high tea or supper in the evening.

Here are some food prices taken from newspaper advertisements in 1926: cocoa 6d (2½p) per ½lb packet; coffee 1/10d (15p) per ½lb; boiled sweets 8d (3½p) per ½lb; liquorice allsorts 1/– (5p) per lb; jam 1/3d (6½p) per jar; canned peaches 10d (4p) per can; bread 9½d (4p) per loaf; and milk 5d (2p) per pint.

25   Bird's Instant Custard powder was as popular in the 1920s as it is today. This advertisement appeared in *The Tatler* in 1928 and is in the style of Mabel Lucie Atwell, a popular children's illustrator.

In 1923 a health craze broke out and Health Food shops opened up in many towns, selling much the same as they do today. Words like "roughage", "balanced diet" and "vitamins" became fashionable. By 1927 the slimming craze had begun and there were all sorts of diets, devices and machines available for the serious slimmer – much like today!

26   This advertisement for the International Stores in 1925 provides information about both food prices and fashion. Notice also the little girl's scooter.

Fruit between Seasons.

Fresh Fruit is delicious but not always obtainable. Canned Fruits of very choice quality can always be purchased at the International and at extremely moderate prices.

large tins.

Apricots   10^d & 1/-

Peaches   11$\frac{1}{2}$^{d} & 1/1

Pears   1/4 & 1/6

small tins

Pineapples   7$\frac{1}{2}$^{d}

Cubes or Slices.

International Stores

The Greatest Grocers in the World

Tea :: Coffee :: Groceries :: Provisions

All International Branches are on the telephone.

5 Schools

The education that many children in the 1920s were receiving was Victorian, in many ways. Schools were housed in old Victorian buildings which were badly equipped and over-crowded. The curriculum was narrow and mainly restricted to the 3Rs. Slowly people were becoming aware that changes were badly needed within the educational system. The main criticism was that most children remained for their entire school-life at the same school, that is, at Elementary School. Secondary schools were available but they were few and far between and fee-paying with large waiting lists. The idea that a secondary education should be a right for every child was gradually gaining strength, though little was actually done about it in the 1920s.

Pre-school children
There were no toddler groups or playgroups to prepare children for school in the 1920s.

Instead, most children had their first experience of school when they walked through the doors of Elementary School, aged 5. (Some private schools had kindergartens which catered for 3-5 year-olds.) In 1922 local authorities were allowed to set up nursery schools if they could afford it, but because of the bad economic climate, few did so. The Hadow Report on Education of 1926 suggested that nurseries be attached to secondary

27   An infants' class in Dallas Road Elementary School, Lancaster, 1925. The schoolroom had not changed since it was built in Victorian times – except that electric lights had been added. The benches are made out of wood and metal and arranged in rows with the teacher in the front. The children are paying into a savings bank. Most schools operated a savings bank scheme; the children had their own savings books and paid in a small amount each Monday morning.

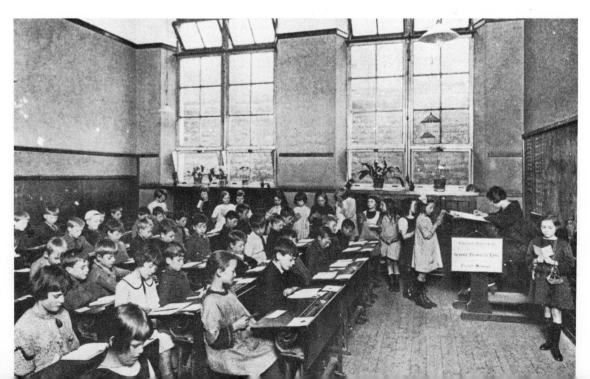

28 This photograph of Roe Lee Council School in Blackburn was taken in 1929. Open-air schools like this were fairly common in the North and were recommended as a means of providing the children from industrial areas with fresh air.

29 The assembly hall of Roe Lee school. Again, this is open on some sides. The children are about to do Drill. What sort of lighting is there?

schools, to give older girls the chance to learn "mothercraft". A few such nurseries were built, but not nearly as many as recommended.

Elementary Schools

95% of the school population went to an Elementary School. Children started at the age of 5 and left at 14, to find a job. Most of these schools were housed in old Victorian buildings which were often badly equipped and poorly ventilated and had no inside lavatories. Few had playing fields or gyms, and some did not even have a playground.

Inside school, girls and boys were segregated, often in separate buildings. Classes were often badly over-crowded, with between 40 and 50 pupils. Sometimes two or three classes had to share one big room and this must have made teaching very difficult.

The 3Rs formed the basis of the curriculum, with Drill (PE) to liven things up. History, Geography, Science and Arts and Crafts were also taught, but less intensively. Gardening, Cookery and Games such as Netball, Hockey, Rounders, Football and Cricket were enjoyed in schools which had adequate facilities. Learning was generally pursued parrot fashion, with little scope for personal expression. However, the situation was not entirely gloomy, for Elementary Schools were free and, on the whole, the standard of teaching was improving as more teachers became trained and certificated.

Secondary Schools

In 1920, 308,000 pupils attended a Secondary School. This included specific Secondary Schools, Grammar Schools and "senior" departments of Elementary Schools. Pupils started at Secondary School aged 11 and left at age 16, having taken the School Certificate examination.

Most children at Secondary School came

30 Listening to the radio was not confined to the home. Boys at Tamworth school in Warwickshire made their own radio during lesson time. They are using headphones.

from middle-class backgrounds, with parents paying an annual fee of between £12 and £13 for their education. 25% of all places at each Secondary School were, theoretically, available free to children from Elementary Schools, providing they won a scholarship. (A qualifying exam was taken at age 11.) Scholarship children were greatly outnumbered and sometimes unjustly regarded as inferior to their fee-paying peers.

Many people were beginning to criticize the "elitism" of the education system. The Hadow Report on Education of 1926 aimed to provide fairer education for each child and recommended that the education system be reorganized to form two stages for all children: Primary from 5 to 11 years and Secondary from 11 to 15 years. This recommendation took many years to be followed up and the new system was not fully in use until the 1940s.

Public and Private Schools

For those parents able to pay, there had always been an alternative education available in the independent sector. Independent schools, which included Public, Private and some Grammar Schools, were not funded by the State, as were Elementary and Secondary Schools, but were run by individuals and paid for by themselves with the help of public subscription. Originally Public Schools had been controlled by public bodies, but over the years they had become expensive, fee-paying schools for the wealthier classes.

Middle-class families often sent their children to a small Private School until they were 11, then on to a fee-paying Secondary School or to another Private or Public School. Wealthier parents sent their children to private kindergartens, preparatory schools and then Public Schools. By 1930 there were 82,000 pupils attending an independent school of one sort or another. Although this was a small minority, their influence was large. Public Schools were still considered to offer the best education and their pupils were

ultimately expected to get the top jobs. Fees were high. In 1925, for example, parents paid £210 a year for the privilege of sending their son to Eton. This was more than a skilled worker earned in a year.

At Public School, life was fairly hard and aimed at being "character-building". Boys were subjected to spartan living conditions, a frugal diet, concentrated learning and rigorous games. The Public School life-style was often idealized in comics such as *The Magnet* which contained stories about Public School where everyone was "chums" and the honour of the school was frequently at stake. The education provided was usually of a high standard, for the "best" masters were attracted to the "best" schools.

There were many Private Schools and a few Public Schools for girls, such as the Cheltenham Ladies' College, but a boy's education was still considered to be more important.

Higher Education

By 1925 61,000 students were receiving a higher education of one form or another, but this was only a small proportion of 18-, 19- and 20-year-olds. Higher education was provided by the Universities, Technical Colleges, Teacher Training Colleges or Evening Institutes (night schools). By 1924 there were 42,000 students at University. This number was almost double the figure at the turn of the century, but only 4 in 1,000 were from an Elementary School background (despite the introduction in 1920 of state-aided scholarships).

Although Oxford and Cambridge were still considered to be the best Universities, the "red brick" ones were also gaining respectability. By 1926, "red bricks" such as Nottingham, Exeter, Hull, Southampton, Leicester and Reading were all offering good degree courses. There was no great competition for places and so, providing a student could pay, he (and occasionally she) could get in to University almost anywhere. Students usually began a three-year degree course at the age of 18 or 19.

In 1920 Oxford made the momentous decision to allow women to read for degrees. (Cambridge did not follow suit until 1948.) Few women went to University, for a specialized training was often considered useless as the vast majority of women gave up work once they got married.

Experimental schools

Several experimental schools were set up in the 1920s. They aimed to encourage a more liberal approach to education. In the education of younger children, Froebel and Montessori were the pioneers. Friedrich Froebel (1782-1852) had opened his first school for infants in 1837 and had encouraged the idea of kindergartens ("children's gardens"). He had believed that learning should be a pleasant experience and that children should be allowed to discover things for themselves. This idea was also expounded by Maria Montessori (1870-1952), who believed that children worked best with little restraint. Several schools based on these beliefs were active in the 1920s.

Similar theories were tried out in schools for older pupils. In 1924 A.S. Neill opened Summerhill, which aimed to "develop hearts not heads". This was followed in 1926 by Dartington Hall, which was also run on progressive lines. Other schools were opened by Rudolf Steiner at Wynstones and by Bertrand Russell and his wife Dora at Frensham Heights. All these schools were co-educational (mixed), and the pupils were encouraged to express themselves freely and expected to do most of the finding out themselves. Although academic subjects were taught, the curriculum was not based on passing examinations. Punishments in the traditional sense were unheard-of. These schools were a small minority and although they definitely worked in some parents' view, many people thought that they were simply "cranky".

Part-timers and truants

The 1918 Education Act had made schooling compulsory for every child until the term in which he or she was 14. However, this was not fully achieved until the Education Act of 1922 which finally put an end to part-time education and, in effect, to child labour. Previously, children in factory areas, such as the textile mills of the North, had worked half the day at school and half the day in the factory. This was now forbidden and, instead, children were limited to doing odd jobs before or after school, such as helping on a milk round or delivering newspapers.

Although education was now compulsory, there were truants. In rural areas, for example, large numbers of children failed to arrive at school when the harvest was being brought in. In towns and villages alike, when an attraction such as a circus arrived, hoards of children would mysteriously disappear! Welfare Officers were meant to keep a sharp eye on truants. The usual punishment, as for everything else, was a caning. If a child regularly missed school, the parents could be taken to court.

Job prospects

As we have seen, the 1920s was a period of high unemployment, especially in the North, Wales and Scotland. For children leaving school in these "depressed" areas the outlook was grim. Children leaving Elementary School at 14 looked for work in shops or factories, or became apprentices or office boys. Many girls went into service. Although the huge army of servants from Victorian days was disappearing fast, many households still had at least one maid or "skivvy". Girls could find jobs as nursery maids, parlour maids, lady's maids, housemaids or cooks. In 1921 there were 1,072,000 girls in service. Other opportunities open for girls included work in shops or factories or as clerical assistants.

Pupils leaving Secondary School aged 16, with a School Certificate, might look for a job in the Civil Service, or in the professions such as teaching, or in local government. Teaching, nursing and secretarial work were possibilities for girls. Once married, 90% of girls, liberated or not, gave up their jobs, for it was still firmly believed that a (married) woman's place was in the home.

31 The office in the Granary Depot of St Pancras Station, 1928. Notice that the clerical workers are all female, evidence that women were successfully taking over what had previously been a male area of work.

6 Family Amusements

Families in the 1920s still relied mainly upon each other for their entertainment. Many people still lived in remote areas and although the radio was becoming more reliable, there was no television. Music was important and many families had a wind-up gramophone which played 78rpm records. Toys and books were also much enjoyed and there was a large range to choose from. By the end of the decade most towns had a cinema as well as some sort of sporting activity.

Music

Many families had a gramophone. Most of them needed to be wound up by hand and had an enormous, horn-shaped loudspeaker. However, by the mid-1920s, electrically operated gramophones were becoming more common. Children could buy mini-versions of the real thing, which either worked by clockwork or could be wound up to play real records. Records were made out of shellac.

Popular songs could be heard on the radio or at the theatre and although there was no chart of "hits", some were much more loved than others. Favourite pop songs in the 1920s included "Swanee" (1920), "Ain't we got fun" (1921), Ma, he's making eyes at me" (1921), "Yes, we have no bananas" (1923), "Tea for Two" (1925), "Show me the way to go home" (1925), "Clap hands, here comes Charlie" (1926), "Bye bye blackbird" (1926) and "Singing in the rain" (1929).

**32 This photograph of Penelope Ethel Morgan ►
was taken in 1922. Dolls and prams were as
popular then as now.**

Toys and books

Many toys that were popular in the 1920s are still enjoyed today. Teddies and dolls came in a variety of shapes and sizes. Board games were enthusiastically played by those who could afford them. Favourite ones were "Snakes and Ladders", "Monopoly", "Ludo" and "Scrabble". Little children played with pull-along toys – wooden animals or figures pulled along by a string. For a few pence, older children could buy tin toys. These were similar to Dinky Toys, and cars, trains and figures were popular. Some toys were clockwork and when wound up, various parts would move. Only

33 This cheeky little doll, typical of the 1920s, is known as a character doll.

Only well-off parents could afford to buy their children an expensive Hornby train set, or Meccano. Really lucky children had sit-in cars which were replicas of real ones. In 1921 pogo sticks became popular and even parents would be seen jumping around on them. They were so fashionable that there was even a song written about them, "Oh! Ogo Pogo".

34 This advertisement for Hamley's toys ► appeared in *The Tatler* in 1928. Although styles have changed, toys today are still basically the same.

34

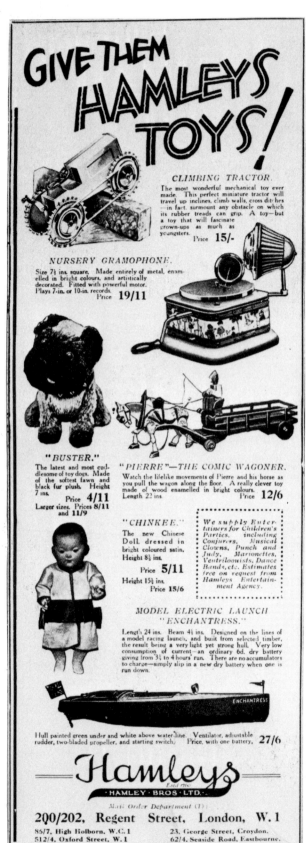

GIVE THEM HAMLEYS TOYS!

CLIMBING TRACTOR.
The most wonderful mechanical toy ever made. This perfect miniature tractor will travel up inclines, climb walls, cross ditches —in fact, surmount any obstacle on which its rubber treads can grip. A toy—but a toy that will fascinate grown-ups as much as youngsters. Price **15/-**

NURSERY GRAMOPHONE.
Size 7½ ins. square. Made entirely of metal, enamelled in bright colours, and artistically decorated. Fitted with powerful motor. Plays 7-in. or 10-in. records. Price **19/11**

"BUSTER."
The latest and most cuddlesome of toy dogs. Made of the softest fawn and black fur plush. Height 7 ins. Price **4/11** Larger sizes. Prices **8/11** and **11/9**

"PIERRE"—THE COMIC WAGONER.
Watch the lifelike movements of Pierre and his horse as you pull the wagon along the floor. A really clever toy made of wood enamelled in bright colours. Length 22 ins. Price **12/6**

"CHINKEE."
The new Chinese Doll, dressed in bright coloured satin. Height 8½ ins. Price **5/11** Height 15½ ins. Price **15/6**

We supply Entertainers for Children's Parties, including Conjurers, Musical Clowns, Punch and Judy, Marionettes, Ventriloquists, Dance Bands, etc. Estimates free on request from Hamleys Entertainment Agency.

MODEL ELECTRIC LAUNCH "ENCHANTRESS."
Length 24 ins. Beam 4½ ins. Designed on the lines of a model racing launch, and built from selected timber, the result being a very light yet strong hull. Very low consumption of current—an ordinary 6d. dry battery giving from 3½ to 4 hours' run. There are no accumulators to charge—simply slip in a new dry battery when one is run down.

Hull painted green under and white above water-line. Ventilator, adjustable rudder, two-bladed propeller, and starting switch. Price, with one battery, **27/6**

Hamleys
HAMLEY BROS LTD.
Estd 1760

Mail Order Department (T):
200/202, Regent Street, London, W.1
85/7, High Holborn, W.C.1
512/4, Oxford Street, W.1
23, George Street, Croydon.
62/4, Seaside Road, Eastbourne.
Oxford Circus Tube Station (Booking Hall).

Many books that were read in the 1920s are still enjoyed today. Popular favourites included *Peter Pan* by J.M. Barrie, *Winnie the Pooh* stories by A.A. Milne, *The Jungle Book* by Rudyard Kipling and the *Just William* books by Richmal Crompton. Children's comics and annuals were also in demand, especially the *Boy's Own* and *Girl's Own* papers and annuals. Little children were not forgotten, for they had the *Little Folk's* annual and a comic called *Tiger Tim*.

Newspapers were keenly read and in 1919 *The Children's Newspaper* was founded by Arthur Mee. Through it, he aimed at presenting all the news in a way that children could understand. At breakfast time, parents might be seen reading from *The Daily Express, The News Chronicle, The Daily Herald, The Daily Mail, The Daily Mirror,* or two of the papers started in the Twenties, *The Daily Telegraph* and *The Daily Sketch*.

Well-stocked family bookshelves might have included books by contemporary writers such as Virginia Woolf, John Galsworthy, Somerset Maugham, Aldous Huxley, H.G. Wells or the controversial James Joyce or D.H. Lawrence. In a lighter vein, P.G. Wodehouse, Agatha Christie and Dorothy Sayers were widely read.

35   Some annuals which were on sale during December 1928. Annuals were popular Christmas presents then as now.

The radio

This invention literally transformed lives in the 1920s and by the end of the decade 85% of the population could listen in. The wireless was first used as a means of sending messages to ships out at sea. It was known as a wireless because the sound was transmitted not by wires but by electromagnetic waves. These messages were soon being picked up by enthusiastic amateurs on their home-made sets. In 1921 a small transmitting station was set up for these amateurs at Writtle, near Chelmsford. This station played a gramophone record every three minutes and was listened to by so many people that in June of the same year Dame Nellie Melba sang at a specially transmitted concert, organized by *The Daily Mail*. In 1922 the rights of broadcast went to the British Broadcasting Company, which, by the following year, was transmitting from stations in London, Birmingham, Manchester, Cardiff, Newcastle and Glasgow. In 1925 the biggest ever station was built at Daventry in Northamptonshire, enabling 85% of the population to tune in.

At first, most people used simple, home-made crystal sets, but soon many radios were being sold. In 1925 a radio cost £25. They were large and clumsy and you generally listened through headphones or a loudspeaker or both. A radio licence cost £10 and by 1930 over 3 million were being issued per year.

For country people the radio was wonderful for they no longer felt so isolated. Now everyone could listen in to hear the same things at the same time. People could also write in with requests. It was a very personal service, with broadcasters being regarded as friends.

The first transmissions were weather forecasts and time signals, but soon "real" programmes were going on the air. By 1923 the BBC was broadcasting for 40 hours a week. This was made up of 3 hours of news, 5½ hours of children's programmes, 45 minutes of religion and the rest of music. From 1926 the BBC was allowed to broadcast daytime news bulletins. (Previously they had had to wait until after 7 pm so as not to upset the newspapers.) By 1927 the BBC (now a Corporation) was also transmitting sporting events such as Wimbledon, the Derby and Henley Regatta. Children had a daily programme known as *Children's Hour*, which went on the air between 5 and 6 pm.

By the end of the decade radios were no longer considered a novelty but were a part of everyday life.

36 *Children's Hour* on the BBC was extremely popular. This is an advertisement for it. Notice the large, heavy radio to which the child is listening through headphones. Radios did not become portable until the 1930s.

Radio programmes for Whit Monday, 1926:
10.30am, Changing of the Guard (live broadcast from Buckingham Palace)
3–5pm, Popular Orchestral programme
5–5.15, *Le Lac* and its author Mme de Walmont
5.15–6, *For the Children*
6–6.40, Talk by the Wireless League
7–7.25, Weather and News Bulletin
7.25–7.40, Mozart Piano Concerto
7.40–8, A.W. Carr (England's Cricket Captain) talking about the Test Match
8–9, Royal Park's Band (live from Hyde Park)
9.30–10, Weather and News Bulletin
10–11, Special Empire Day Programme
11, Closedown

Girl Guides and Boy Scouts
Both these movements were very popular in the Twenties. The Boy Scout movement had been formed in 1907 by Baden Powell, and this had been followed closely by the formation of the Girl Guides in 1910. As well as having

weekly meetings, groups of children could spend holidays at camps where they learned to look after themselves and help others. A worldwide Jamboree of Boy Scouts was held at Birkenhead in 1929.

Sports

It seems that everyone, young or old, was interested in one sport or another in the 1920s. The most popular spectator sport was football. Every Saturday afternoon entire families would go to watch a local football match. In 1925 the Playing Fields Association was set up to provide more sports fields, and a network of

37 The Mill Garden Brownies from Sydenham, London, at their annual camp in 1924. The uniform has changed a little since then, but the spirit has not!

38 Football was the greatest spectator sport of the 1920s. Aston Villa were cup winners during 1919/20, and attracted large crowds.

amateur leagues was established throughout the country.

Tennis was also popular and the Wimbledon championships were enthusiastically attended by those who could afford to. Suzanne Lenglen revolutionized women's play by wearing short dresses with no stockings and by playing over-arm! She was the Ladies' Champion from 1919-25. Tennis clubs started and public courts were built in parks.

Swimming was fashionable and many open-air and indoor pools were opened. Some children were taken for weekly swimming lessons by their schools.

The Boat Race between Oxford and Cambridge was a popular event during the 1920s and literally thousands of people turned up every year to watch it, usually dressed in either light or dark blue, depending on which crew they supported. Special flags were made for children to wave and even Boat Race cakes were baked, decorated in shades of blue. The most dramatic race of the decade was in 1924 when the Oxford boat sank.

The Olympic Games of 1920, 1924 and 1928 were all closely listened to on the radio, and for the first time many women were among the participants.

Other popular sports included ice-skating (again, many rinks opened and were used by families), dirt-track motor-bike racing and greyhound racing (the first track opened in Belle Vue in Manchester in 1926). For the more genteel, rambling and picnicking appealed.

39 **This family is relaxing in the garden of their home in Finchley. It is Sunday afternoon and the men are playing an energetic game of Kumbak tennis (still in their "Sunday best"). Other members of the family laze in the sun, while a little girl is playing with a pull-along toy.**

7 Holidays and Fun

After the war people seemed anxious to enjoy themselves and their almost frantic pursuit of fun has given the period the nickname of the "Roaring Twenties". Although a minority, because of terrible circumstances, were not able to benefit from it, mass entertainment flourished as never before and was usually cheap and very cheerful. The cinema had its heyday in the 1920s and was always well-attended by all age-groups. Holidays were beginning to be considered a right rather than a privilege, although few fathers had paid annual leave. Crazes, usually imported from America, swept through the country — for instance, crossword puzzles, introduced in 1924, the board game "Mah Jong", and Whist and Bridge. And everyone was dancing!

Dancing

Every year new dances were brought to Britain from America. Most of these

40 The Charleston arrived from America in 1925 and was one of the most popular dances of the period. It was considered very risqué in its day. The girls are being taught the dance by the oddly dressed character on the left.

profoundly shocked the older generation, for young people no longer danced sedately together but danced vigorously at each other! The most famous 1920s' dance was the Charleston, but there were other equally energetic dances including the "Shimmy", the "Black Bottom", the "Camel", the "Twinkle", the "Jog Trot" and the "Vampire"! For the "Bright Young Things" dancing was vital and they whiled away their days in Palais de Danse. Children started off by learning ballroom dances such as the Waltz and Foxtrot and progressed to Ballet or Tap before launching into popular dances.

The cinema

The cinema, or Picture Palace as it was known,

was extremely popular. Most families went at least once a week and loved everything that was on, from the Comedies to the "Weepies". There was usually a special Saturday morning show for children. The bill lasted for three hours and cost less than 1s (5p).

At first, all films were silent. Words were usually shown in between the pictures so that you knew what was going on. In smart cinemas the film was accompanied by music played on an electric organ or even by an

41   The cinema enjoyed a heyday in the 1920s. This one proudly advertised talking pictures in 1929.

orchestra. In the local "flea pit" a piano was the norm.

Favourite films included swashbucklers such as *Robin Hood* (1922) and *Ben Hur* (1926) and romances such as *The Sheik* (1921), starring the much-loved Rudolph Valentino. Comedies were also much appreciated, especially if the star was Charlie Chaplin or Buster Keaton. Animated cartoons made their first appearance in 1925 with Felix the Cat. He was soon followed by Bonzo the Dog and in 1928 by the most famous of them all, Mickey Mouse.

In 1928, the first "talkies" arrived, though not everyone thought they would catch on. The first talking film was *The Jazz Singer*, which starred Al Jolson. It caused a sensation and heralded a new era in the cinema.

Theatres

With the arrival of the cinema and its phenomenal success, fewer people went to the theatre. However, many successful and well-known plays were produced during the Twenties. Theatre was generally "light" and escapist. People loved the glittering revues of C.B. Cochran and the somewhat black comedies of Noel Coward. Thrillers, farces and drawing-room comedies were all much enjoyed, as were musicals written by such people as Gershwin and Cole Porter. Popular shows in this genre included *Rose Marie* (1925), *No, no Nanette* (1925), *The Aldwych Farces* (1928) and *Private Lives* (1930). Serious plays were also written by authors such as George Bernard Shaw, Somerset Maugham and John Galsworthy. For children there was the annual Christmas pantomime and the yearly production of *Peter Pan*.

Variety Theatres were also loved by families. These usually offered a mixed programme of different acts. During the summer, holidaymakers flocked to see the end of the pier show, and in the country, amateur dramatic groups produced plays and pantomimes in village halls.

Holidays

In the 1920s people in work were not automatically entitled to paid leave. Those who took holidays were not usually paid during the time they were away. The vast

42 This charabanc was photographed in 1925 outside the Worcester Brine Baths Hotel. Charabancs were a popular means of travelling and could hold up to 40 people and their luggage. When it rained or was cold, the roof could be pulled up from the back.

43 This Caravan was built in 1923 and was called an "Angela". Inside there was a pull-out double bed, a pull-out table and several cupboards. It was lit by oil lamps and cooking was done on a small stove.

majority of people worked all the year round, but slowly the idea that holidays were good for you was becoming more acceptable. Those who could afford to went to the seaside for a week.

Others went just for a day trip, perhaps in a charabanc. Wealthier families went abroad, to places like Switzerland or Brittany.

Most people stayed in bed-and-breakfast places or in hotels. Others took a caravan with them. Caravans had been on the market since 1919 but were not mass-produced until 1922 when the Eccles trailer was manufactured.It was motorized and looked like a gypsy caravan but without the horse!

On the beach, families often hired bathing

44 Two sisters enjoying a family holiday at West Bay, Dorset, in 1926. Notice their legged bathing costumes, cloche-style rubber caps and rubber bathing shoes. (In the background bathing huts are just visible.)

45 The author's father enjoying a donkey ride in ➤ 1929. Notice that the children appear to be wearing their school uniform.

huts. Here you could store all your clothes, chairs and other belongings and even cook a meal. Sunbathing was popular for the first time and bathing costumes became a little more revealing. They were still covered-up by today's standards. Children changed under voluminous towelling robes which had drawstring necks. They wore rubber bathing hats, and macintosh paddlers on their feet to protect them from sharp rocks.

The scene would be familiar, with deckchairs and umbrellas, buckets and spades, ice-creams and sandy sandwiches, donkey rides and Punch and Judy – only the people were rather more decorous in their dress. Children from the slums, however, were unlikely ever to enjoy the delights of a holiday.

8 Transport

Huge developments were made in transport during the Twenties and, generally, most families could afford to use one form or another. Cars were very popular. They were mass-produced and therefore cheap. They brought with them new problems of pollution, traffic control and road safety, but most people were aware only of their advantages. For those who could not afford a car, a motor-cycle was a good alternative. In towns, buses and trams gave an efficient service. In the skies the aeroplane captured everyone's imagination.

Cars

During the Twenties cars came within the reach of ordinary people and were obviously not a passing craze as many sceptics had forecast. There was no driving test and anyone

46   The Austin 7 was one of the most popular and cheap of all cars of the 1920s. One of its drawbacks was that it sometimes had to be driven up-hill backwards! If it were driven forwards, oil might flood the carburettor and stall the engine.

47 Two children posing in front of their family's first-ever car, bought in 1926. The car is a Bean, made by A. Harper, Sons and Bean. This particular car was bought to take the family on holiday and accommodated three adults, two children and their picnic basket. The luggage still had to go by rail. Any petrol needed for the journey was carried with them in cans (petrol stations being few and far between).

over the age of 16 could buy a licence. By 1930 there were over one million privately owned cars on the roads. The most popular type was the Austin 7 which cost £122 in 1922. At the other end of the scale was the princely Rolls Royce which sold at £2,925 in 1923. Other favourite makes included the Morris Minor, Morris Cowley and the Model T Ford ("Tin Lizzie"). Although some of these cars had

electric starters, many of them still needed a crank start.

Roads were totally unequipped to cope with this new phenomenon, as were most people. There was no highway code and although the speed limit was fixed at 20mph, no-one took any notice of it. There were many accidents. In 1930, for example, there was a total of 156,000 accidents, 7,000 of which were fatal. Society became divided into "pedestrians" and "motorists", and fast, careless drivers were known as "road hogs". By 1926, the first traffic lights were in use. Other precautions included hand signals and hooting the horn when going around a corner.

Not everyone loved cars. Some people were worried that they would spoil the countryside as more and more motorists headed out to find rural beauty spots. Others were concerned about pollution and the changes cars were enforcing on towns. Others mourned the inevitable decline of horse power in its true sense.

Bicycles and motor-cycles

Pedal cycles enjoyed a boom. Children started off with a tricycle. These were larger than today's and a child rode it until the age of 8 or 9, then progressed to a Fairy Cycle, which was an ordinary two-wheeler. Scooters and go-carts were also popular with children. Until 1930 anyone over the age of 14 could buy a motor-cycle licence and by that year there were over 720,000 motor-cycles on the roads. (In 1930 the age limit was fixed at 16.) Many motor-cycles had sidecars. A passenger or even two small children could squeeze in and ride along with the motor-cyclist. There was also room for a pillion passenger.

Trains

No new railways were built in the 1920s and the only main change was the amalgamation of hundreds of tiny railway companies into four major ones. These were the Great Western; The London, Midland and Scottish; The London and North Eastern; and The Southern. This led to standardization and

48 Another cheap means of transport. Sidecars for motor-cycles were very common.

49 Hendon Central Station was opened in 1924 as part of the London Underground extension. The coaches were painted scarlet and cream and the Underground boasted that it gave "clean, swift travel".

THE PROBLEM OF THE
UNDERGROUND

1923 REQUIRED

COAL 234,000 TONS

OIL 71,000 GALLONS

STAFF 10,000

STEEL & IRON 6,000 TONS

TICKETS 200 TONS

TAXES £184,000

WHAT IT TAKES TO
MOVE THE PASSENGERS

306,000,000

TRAVELLED IN 1923

50 This poster combines facts with an attractive design. The statistics are interesting. How do you think they compare with today's figures?

51 Companies such as the Berkshire Aviation Company were popular throughout the Twenties. They gave flying exhibitions all round the country, with the pilot doing stunts such as wing-walking. They also gave joy-rides. In three years the Berkshire Aviation Company had flown 337,000 people, for a guinea (£1.10p) a go. This plane is an Avro 505K and was painted red and silver. The pilot is the author's grandfather.

greater efficiency. All trains were powered by steam and could travel at up to 70 mph.

In London the Underground system was expanded to meet the needs of growing suburbia. In 1924 new lines to Hendon in the north and Morden in the south were opened.

Aeroplanes

The 1920s was the decade of flying adventures.

Records were broken, new planes designed and passenger routes opened. The popular imagination was well and truly captured! Solo flights were made across the Atlantic and to Australia, and names such as Alcock, Brown and Lindberg became well-known throughout the country.

There were public flying displays and many companies gave joy-rides. In 1919 Aircraft Travel and Transport Ltd launched the first international service from Hounslow to Paris. The fare was 15 guineas (£15.75) single. The service was then extended to Amsterdam, Brussels, Manchester, Belfast and the Channel Islands. In 1924 Imperial Airways was formed and operated flights to the European capitals. By 1929, this company was offering a service to India. The trip to Delhi took eight days and passengers travelled in aeroplane, train and flying boat. By modern standards, conditions aboard were very basic.

Each plane could hold only a few passengers, say four or six, and only the sophisticated offered lavatory and buffet services.

Airships

At first, airships were considered to be workable alternatives to aeroplanes. In 1919 the R34 was built. It was over 213 metres long and travelled at 60 mph. It needed a crew of 60 to look after 40 passengers, but was meant to offer a very smooth and quiet ride. Popular enthusiasm was dampened when the R34 broke up in mid-air in 1921, killing most of its crew.

There was a lack of interest until 1929-30 when two new ships were built. These were the R100 and R101. They were meant to be faster,

52 This is what the inside of a passenger plane looked like in 1929. This plane was one of the fleet of the Imperial Airways and was considered very comfortable. Amenities included six passenger seats, two lavatories, baggage space and buffet. There was no air hostess but the plane was flown by two pilots.

safer, more economical and more luxurious. In October 1930 the R101 started on its first major flight, to India, when it lost height over the coast of France and exploded. Only six people out of fifty-four survived. Public shock was great and all hopes for the future of airship travel evaporated.

9 Town Life

Town life saw significant changes during the 1920s, almost entirely due to the motorization of vehicles. The sights, sounds and smells in towns all changed. Roads had to be altered or new ones built to accommodate more traffic. The air was now filled with the sound of motor engines and horns and the pungent smell of horses was being replaced by exhaust fumes. However, as transport improved, more and more people came into towns for their work, shopping and social life. More families came to live in towns and this influx compounded the general housing shortage and led to much urban expansion into the suburbs.

53   Market day at Salisbury in the mid-1920s. Notice the charabancs and omnibuses. Some of the lorries are being used as stalls, with drapes fixed over their rear doors.

Roads

Traffic jams and congestion were a frequent sight in most towns. In 1929 a census taken at Blackfriars Bridge in London revealed that the following traffic crossed the bridge in one day between the hours of 8 am and 8 pm: 2,568 electric trams, 1,548 omnibuses, 7,399 light cars (private), 2,397 heavy cars (commercial), 2,898 horse-drawn vehicles, 270 motor-cycles, 2,292 pedal cycles and 244 barrows. Not only is that a striking amount of traffic but also it shows the great variety of vehicles being used. Notice the still large numbers of horse-drawn vehicles. They were used mainly by people such as milkmen, coalmen and rag-and-bone men.

There were no road markings but most roads were heavily criss-crossed with tram lines. The roads were swept regularly and children would often follow behind horses and carts to scoop up any offerings that the horse might have left!

54 This photograph of London Bridge, taken in 1929, gives a good impression of how much traffic was on the roads, and of the general confusion. There are private cars, horse-drawn vans, open and covered buses, commercial lorries, hand carts and pedestrians. Notice the absence of lines on the road and of any other road signs, but a new telephone box is on the left and there are some attractive street lights.

Street furniture

Many streets were now lit by electric lights, although gas lighting was still in use in some country towns. In 1923 the neon light first made an appearance and brightened up cities with its lively signs.

In 1926 the first red telephone kiosks were introduced. Previously towns had all used different designs. The new kiosks were designed by Sir Gilbert Scott and were originally made out of cast iron. This was later

55 Outside a small grocer's shop. Notice the ▶ ornate moulding on the shop window and the pretty lettering. The left-hand side seems to be devoted to dried fruit and the right-hand side to meat.

replaced by pre-fabricated concrete. Not everyone liked them. The people of Eastbourne, for example, thought their original thatched kiosks far more in keeping with their then rural environment. Letterboxes were also red and of a similar design to today's.

In 1926 the first traffic lights appeared and helped ease the traffic congestion a little. Metal signs advertising everything from Oxo to sewing machines were to be seen all over walls and shop fronts. Most of them were attractive and they are now collectors' items.

Shops

Generally speaking, shops were smaller and

56 A small greengrocer's in Warwick in 1921. Notice that the goods are displayed in baskets on the pavement. Would this be allowed today?
▼

57 Inside a ladies' dress shop. Articles on sale range from umbrellas on the left to fox furs in the display cabinet.

more packed with goods than today and provided a friendly, personal service. In high streets we would recognize such names as Marks and Spencer, Woolworth's, Boots the Chemist, Freeman, Hardy and Willis, International Stores, British Home Stores, Burton's and the Co-op. Although the trend was towards larger shops, many small, specialist shops still flourished and even the smallest street was likely to have a corner shop selling everything. Window dressing was considered an art and competitions were held locally and nationally to find the best display in various fields. Frequently shops such as greengrocers' displayed their goods in baskets on the pavements, while others such as butchers' hung their wares on exterior walls.

For the thirsty shopper there were plenty of cafes to choose from. Lyons Corner Houses offered tasty food at reasonable prices. Their waitresses, known as "Nippies", were the first to serve American-style blocks of ice-cream, in 1923. The Kardomah Coffee House chain also offered good value for money.

Street traders
Street traders and hawkers were numerous and worked either on foot with a hand-barrow, or with a horse and cart. Each individual

usually had a distinctive street call by which his customers would recognize him. Common sights included Italian ice-cream sellers, or hokey-pokey (water-ice) men as they were sometimes called, rag-and-bone men, knife-grinders, fish-sellers and tinkers. Even muffin men and cats' meat sellers were still in evidence in the Twenties.

Public transport

In towns, public transport was divided between the trams and the omnibuses. Trams were Victorian inventions and had been pulled originally by horses. By the Twenties they were electric and ran either on an overhead wiring system or on tracks which electrified as the tram went over them. Trams were not steered but simply followed the direction of the tramlines, the driver controlling the speed and braking. When reaching the terminus, the driver and conductor swopped ends and the backs of the passenger seats were tipped to

58 Part of an advertisement for United Dairies in 1927, showing a London milkman. The horse-drawn vans were orange and the United Dairies prided themselves on their smart appearance and healthy product. Milk arrived from the country in glass-lined milk-tanks on the backs of lorries. It was then pasteurized, bottled and delivered.

59 Dustmen in most towns went about with a horse and cart, but electrically operated sanitary collecting carts like these were becoming more widespread after 1924. They were designed by Shelvoke and Drewry of Letchworth.

60 The staff of the Midland Red Omnibus Company posing outside their Leamington Spa depot in 1923.

face the other direction. The tram then returned the way it had come. The trams could be single- or double-decked, with an open or covered top. Most were colourfully painted in the town's livery and were covered in advertising slogans.

Trams were cheap, plentiful and reliable, but by the end of the 1920s were slowly being replaced by omnibuses. Both omnibuses and trams were run by local authorities, such as City Councils, but there were also private omnibus companies which offered a competitive service in towns and between towns. At first, omnibuses were open to the skies and each seat on the top deck had a waterproof bib attached to it which could be pulled over your knees should it rain during the journey. By the end of the decade most omnibuses were covered. In 1926 the Victoria Omnibus Station opened in London, specializing in long-distance travel.

10 Country Life

Enormous changes were also taking place in the countryside during the Twenties. The sleepiness of pre-war rural England was shattered by the arrival of the motor-car, as trips to country beauty spots became a popular pastime amongst townspeople. Mass production of goods and the ease of getting into towns brought an end to the traditional self-

61 This photograph of Burton Bradstock was taken in the early 1920s. Burton Bradstock must have been typical of many rural villages. The building on the right is the post office and village store. Note the motor-cycle and sidecar in the foreground, and the horse and cart in the background.

62 Although many traditional crafts were dying out, many villages still had a blacksmith who not only shod horses but also coped with any iron-mongery problem. This is a typical interior of a smithy.

sufficiency of villages and this resulted in the decline of many rural crafts. Motor-bus services allowed more people to go into towns for their jobs and entertainment. On the good side, many country homes no longer felt isolated from the rest of the world as improvements in transport and general amenities widened their horizons.

Community life
Pre-war villages had been tight-knit, often self-sufficient communities, with people rarely travelling more than a few miles away.

63 Vans like this travelled throughout the ▶ country, bringing fresh bread and cakes to the village shop or to housewives' doors. Many country women, of course, still baked their own bread.

This was all changing. Many amenities such as travelling shops and even libraries started to reach remote villages, but also more people were leaving to find work in towns. Rural industries such as saddlers and cart-makers declined, as cheap, mass-produced goods became available. However, the picture was not entirely gloomy, for moves were made to

64 This photograph of a waggoner's yard shows how country people relied on both horse-drawn and motor vehicles. Here maize is being loaded on to the carts.

protect the countryside and to keep communities together. There was a spate of village hall building. The halls were used for occasions such as public meetings and drama events. New clubs such as the Young Farmers (founded 1921) and the Women's Institute (founded 1915) encouraged village pride. Most villages still had their school, and some still had their Hiring Fair. These fairs were held annually and farm labourers would put themselves up for hire for a year to any farmer who wanted them. There were booths and stalls and an ox roast. Some fairs are still held today, but only from a funfair point of view.

Farming

Great changes were taking place in farming. Livestock was becoming more popular than arable, though sugar-beet-growing was encouraged by a government subsidy. There was a move towards mechanization, though horses were still in common use. In 1925 the Ferguson light tractor came into production, a machine which would eventually bring about the end of working horses. Battery hens made poultry more productive and there was an increase in market gardening as a result of the flourishing canning industry. The most popular vegetable for canning was peas, and the favourite fruits were raspberries, strawberries and plums.

After the war there was a shortage of labour and many farms had fallen into neglect. The labourers there were, worked long, hard hours for poor wages. Compulsory education and, in 1922, the end of part-timing for children (half their time spent at school and half at work) meant that children could no longer be relied on to help out with small jobs such as bird-scaring, clearing the fields of stones or bean-

65   The majority of farmers relied exclusively on horses for heavy work. This horse team is ploughing on a farm in Ravenstonedale, Cumbria.

66 Tractors were becoming more widespread towards the end of the Twenties. This photograph shows a farmer harrowing with a Cumberland-registration tractor, on Crossgill Farm, Garrigill, County Durham.

picking. Many children did, however, truant from school during harvest time.

Country homes

Progress was slower in the country than in the towns. By 1929 only 3% of farms had electricity. Most homes were lit by gas, oil lamps or candles. Few farms had an indoor water supply – water was fetched from a pump in the yard. Heating was by open fires and cooking was done on the range.

Many villages did have post offices and some even had a telephone kiosk. A shop and a pub completed the picture. Door-to-door salesmen were common. They sold everything from trinkets and material to pots and pans. Milk

was delivered daily and the fishman supplied ice for ice boxes.

Country pleasures

Weekending in the country became popular with well-off families. Some even bought a country cottage (usually to the loss of the farm labourer who could no longer afford what was traditionally his). Motoring and cycling in the country were enjoyed and the Cycling Tourist Club founded in 1878 had a large following in the Twenties. By the end of the decade, Youth Hostelling was making a start in the Lake District and in Wales. This was a German idea

67 A favourite pastime for town people was to picnic in the countryside, usually at weekends. Picnics were well-organized; these couples have come equipped with tables, chairs and hamper. Notice the caravan in the background of this Underground poster.

German idea which was to become very popular in the Thirties.

Concern about the safety of villages and the countryside led to the founding of the Council for the Preservation of Rural England in 1926, a society which is still active today.

11 People in the News

As we have seen, newspapers were avidly read during the 1920s. They, along with the radio, were the main source of news, for remember that television was only in its infancy. As today, politics, unusual incidents at home and abroad, entertainment, sport and the goings-on of famous people took up most of the space. This chapter gives brief biographies of a few of the people who appeared fairly regularly in the news in the 1920s for their achievements and activities. For more details of these people and others of the period look in the biography section of your local library.

John Logie Baird (1888-1946)

Born in Helensburgh, Dumbartonshire, John Logie Baird was the son of a rector. He followed an engineering course at the Royal Technical College in Glasgow, and then went on to Glasgow University. By the early 1920s he was researching into television. His first television consisted of a tea-chest motor, a projection light made out of an old biscuit tin and scanning discs made out of cardboard. It was all assembled on a washstand in his bedroom. His first major success was made in 1924 when he transmitted the image of a Maltese Cross. In 1925 he came to London and lived in a state of ill-health and poverty. The following year he gave his first television demonstration to a group of scientists and in the same year Baird Television Development Company Ltd was formed. In 1928 this company made the first television transmission between London and New York. In 1932 the BBC took over programmes previously handled by Baird's company, and he concentrated on the big screen and colour. In 1937 he became the first Briton to receive the Gold Medal from the International Faculty of Science.

Stanley Baldwin (1867-1947)

Born in Bewdley, Worcestershire, Stanley Baldwin was educated at Harrow and Cambridge. In 1908 he succeeded his father as MP for Bewdley and by 1922 had become Chancellor of the Exchequer. The following year he was recognized as Leader of the House of Commons, and when Bonar-Law resigned, Stanley Baldwin became Prime Minister in May. Although defeated in the General Election of November 1923, he remained leader of the Conservative Party. When the Labour Government fell in 1924 he again became Prime Minister and two years later safely led the country through the General Strike. Although his Government was again defeated in 1929, he still retained leadership of the Conservatives and in 1931 became Lord President of the Council. He was Prime Minister again from 1935-37, during the difficult period leading up to the Second World War. He also saw the country through the Abdication Crisis of 1935. On his resignation in 1937, Baldwin received a knighthood. He was modest, patriotic and ruled with quiet authority and was loved by politicians and ordinary people alike.

Margaret Bondfield (1873-1953)

Margaret Bondfield was born in Chard, Somerset, the tenth of eleven children. She was an avid reader and became very interested

68 Margaret Bondfield on the platform with Ramsay MacDonald at a Labour Party meeting in 1924.

in women's rights. Her first jobs were as a shop assistant and in 1894 she joined the Shop Assistants Union, eventually becoming its assistant secretary. In 1899 she was the first woman delegate at the Trade Union Congress, and later became its President in 1923, again the first woman to do so. She was also a member of the Fabian Society and of several organizations concerned with women's rights including the Women's Labour League and the Women's Co-operative Guild. In 1923 she became MP for Northampton, representing the Labour Party, and was later MP for Wallsend from 1926-31. She attained a further distinction by becoming the first woman Cabinet Minister when she was given the post of Minister of Labour in Ramsay MacDonald's Government of 1929. She continued her interests in the Trade Union movement and women's rights until her death.

Neville Chamberlain (1869-1940)

Born in Birmingham, Neville Chamberlain studied metallurgy and engineering at Mason Court (Birmingham University). In 1890, he went to the Bahamas to manage his father's estates but after several years of hard work he found them uneconomic and returned to Birmingham. Here he became a member of the City Council, and held the office of Lord Mayor. He became a notable figure and one of his many achievements was to found the first municipal savings bank. In 1918 he became MP for Ladywood and eventually became Chancellor of the Exchequer in 1923. Here he concentrated on reforming the old Poor Law, and providing new houses to cope with the shortage. In the 1929 Election he became MP for Edgbaston, a post he held until his death. In May 1937 he succeeded Baldwin as Prime Minister and held the position during the turbulent period leading up to the Second World War, and it is for this that he is most known.

Charlie Chaplin (1889-1977)

Charlie Chaplin was born in Kennington, London and made his first stage appearance at a London Music Hall at the age of five. He joined a touring acting troupe and in 1913 went to America with them. Here he joined Mack Senet's Keystone Company and made his screen debut in 1914 playing an English dandy. By 1915, he had adopted his famous guise of the tramp with the ill-fitting suit, bowler hat and cane, shuffling walk and pancake make-up. He was an immediate success and was soon writing and directing his own particular blend of slapstick comedy combined with pathos. His best films include *The Kid* (1921), *The Gold Rush* (1925), *City Lights* (1931) and *Modern Times* (1935). He loved working in mime, and disliked "talkies". In 1953 he was exiled from America because of rumours attached to his private life and alleged communism, and thereafter he lived mainly in Switzerland. He made his last film in 1967 – *A Countess from Hongkong*. He was knighted in 1975.

Sir Alan Cobham (1894-1973)

During the First World War he served as a pilot in the Flying Corps, and entered the realm of civil aviation in 1920. At first, he specialized in aerial photography but it soon became clear that he had a true pioneer nature and almost inexhaustible energy. He made several "firsts" in aviation and flew all over the world. His achievements include flying to India and back in 1924, Cape Town and back in 1925 and in 1926 he not only made a return trip to Australia, but also went on a flying boat expedition around the entire African continent. In 1931 his famous Flying Circus took to the air and toured Great Britain. It is estimated that the Circus gave 1,250 air displays and carried 900,000 passengers on short trips. Sir Alan Cobham was also a pioneer in the refuelling of aircraft in mid-air. Apart from all this, he also had time to write several books and many magazine articles. He was also the subject of several films.

Al Jolson (1888-1950)

Al Jolson was born in St Petersburg, Russia, as Asa Yoelson. His family emigrated to America in 1895 and Al began his career as a stage extra in a New York Variety Theatre. In 1899 he blacked his face and formed a minstrel troupe. This was so successful that he was "discovered" and brought to Hollywood. He specialized in sentimental songs delivered in a very melodramatic way. He achieved much recognition by being the star in the first "talkie", *The Jazz Singer*, in 1927. His other films include *Mammy* (1930) and *Rhapsody in Blue* (1945).

Suzanne Lenglen (1899-1935)

Suzanne Lenglen was born in France and became one of the most popular and talented women tennis players. She won her first championship in 1914 at St Cloud in France, and from 1919-23, and again in 1925, she was Ladies' Champion at Wimbledon. She revolutionized women's tennis by playing over-arm and generally attacking the game in a masculine style, which in turn raised the standard. She also adopted short skirts and no stockings and was famous for the bandeau she wore to keep her hair out of her eyes. She had a glamorous and dynamic style and was much admired. In 1926 she turned professional, and also ran a coaching school in Paris. After her early death from anaemia, huge crowds attended her funeral. She was awarded the posthumous Cross of the Légion d'Honneur.

Charles Lindbergh (1902-74)

Charles Lindbergh was born in Detroit,

69 Captain Lindbergh addressing a crowd at Croydon aerodrome.

America. In 1926 he became an air-mail pilot, flying from Chicago to St Louis. The following year he became a popular hero by making the first solo non-stop transatlantic flight from New York to Paris. He flew in a monoplane called the *Spirit of St Louis* and the 3,610-mile journey took him 33½ hours. After this, he toured many American cities promoting aeronautics. He also worked with Dr A. Carel on physiological experiments. He married Anne Morrow, but his family life was forever clouded by the abduction and murder of his infant son in 1932.

Dame Nellie Melba (1861-1931)
Helen Mitchell (Dame Nellie's real name) was born in Melbourne, Australia, into a musical family. From a young age, she studied the piano and organ. In 1882 she married Charles Armstrong, but her marriage was so unhappy that in 1886 her father paid her passage to England. At first, her singing was not well-received by the English, and she went to Paris to be taught by the famous instructor, Madame Mathilde Marchesi. In 1887 she made her operatic debut in *Rigoletto* and immediately was a great success. By now she had adopted her stage name of Nellie Melba (taken from Melbourne) and travelled to many capitals of the world gaining great popularity. In 1921 she was the first artiste to have a concert broadcast from the early experimental radio station at Writtle, near Chelmsford. In 1918 she was created a Dame of the British Empire (DBE). She has also left her mark upon cuisine, for Peach Melba and Melba toast are both named after her!

James Ramsay MacDonald (1866-1937)
Born in Lossiemouth, Morayshire, Ramsay MacDonald came from an impoverished farming family. He started work as a pupil teacher at his old school, and in 1885 moved to Bristol where he joined the Social Democratic Federation. He eventually moved to London where he suffered from bad health and poverty and existed by doing any job he could find. In

1894 he joined the Labour Party and was its secretary from 1900-12. In 1906 he became MP for Leicester and quickly established a reputation in the House of Commons. During the First World War he was a pacifist and this attitude lost him popularity and his seat. In 1922 he was returned as MP for Aberfan and was now seen as the official Leader of the Opposition. In 1924 he became Prime Minister of the first Labour Government and, due to his knowledge of foreign affairs, also held the post of Foreign Secretary. He was defeated at the General Election of October 1924, mainly as a result of the bogus " Zinoviev letter" and its implications of Bolshevism. He played a major part in drafting the Labour Party manifesto which was published in 1928. In 1929 he again became Prime Minister, and from 1931-35 retained this position in the Coalition Government. In 1937 he held the position of Lord President of the Council but was forced to resign through ill-health. Upon his death, he was given a state funeral in Westminster Abbey and buried at Lossiemouth.

Sir Ernest Shackleton (1874-1922)
Ernest Shackleton was born in Kilkee, County Kildare. He was educated at Dulwich College and went to sea as an apprentice. In 1901 he was a junior officer on Scott's National Antarctic expedition. He became obsessed by a desire to reach the South Pole and made two expeditions in 1907 and 1914. During the latter expedition, his ship, the *Endurance*, was trapped in ice and he and five companions made an astonishing 800-mile journey to safety, eventually arriving in South Georgia. He wrote an account of this incredible trip in his book, *South*. In September 1921 he set sail in the *Quest* on another Antarctic expedition but died suddenly at South Georgia. He was a man of great courage and leadership, with a huge love of adventure. His achievements were recognized by several medals and a knighthood. After his death, there was a memorial service for him in St Paul's

70 Sir Ernest Shackleton, 1921.

Cathedral which was attended by members of the Royal Family.

Rudolph Valentino (1895-1926)

Rudolph Valentino was born in Italy. Having graduated from the Royal Academy of Agriculture in Genoa, he saw few prospects for himself in Italy and emigrated to America in 1913. His first job was as a professional dancing partner, but his talents were recognized and by 1917 he had arrived in Hollywood. The film *The Four Horsemen of the Apocalypse* catapulted him to fame, and he was soon being admired for his smouldering good looks and romantic image. He was perhaps best-loved for his portrayal of *The Sheik* in 1921. His brief career was ended in 1926 by a perforated ulcer. At his funeral, thousands of women mourned him and there were scenes of mass hysteria.

Date List

1919   Alcock and Brown make the first direct flight across the Atlantic (June).
Addison's Housing Act: the Government subsidizes houses built by local authorities.
The Children's Newspaper founded by Arthur Mee.
Lady Astor elected as the first woman MP.

1920   Conscription abolished (April).
League of Nations set up.
Women allowed to take degrees at Oxford University for the first time.
The Communist Party of Great Britain founded.
Broadcasting tests begin at Marconi Ltd in Writtle.
Coal Strike from October to November.

1921   Post-War Depression.
Coal Strike from April to July.
The Railway Act merges hundreds of small companies into four major ones.
The Education Act provides free milk for needy children.
Ernest Shackleton sets sail for the Antarctic.
R38 airship crashes (August).
Artificial silk on the market for the first time.
The All Electric House on display at the Daily Mail Exhibition.
Irish Free State founded (December).

1922   2 million on the dole; hunger marches in protest.
Benito Mussolini PM of Italy.
Sir Eric Geddes, head of Government Committee, recommends big cuts in government spending; the consequent measures known as "Geddes Axe".
Discovery of insulin by Banting and Best.
Civil War in Southern Ireland.
Education Act prohibits part-time education and effectively ends any possibilities of child labour.
Lloyd George resigns; Bonar-Law becomes Prime Minister (October).
British Broadcasting Company founded (December).

1923   Marriage of Lady Elizabeth Bowes-Lyons to the future George VI (April).
Bonar-Law resigns; Stanley Baldwin becomes PM (May).
Discovery of Tutankhamun's tomb by Lord Carnarvon.
Craze for "bobbed" hair begins.
Work starts on the extension of the London Underground.
Radio Times first published (September).
First FA Cup Final, at Wembley.
Hitler writes *Mein Kampf*, which becomes the Nazi political statement.

General Election in December; Minority Conservative Government voted in, but to remain in power recruits support of developing Labour Party.

1924   Ramsay MacDonald becomes Prime Minister with first Labour Government (January).
British Empire Exhibition at Wembley opened by King George V.
Commercial Treaty with Russia.
Imperial Airways formed.
First BBC broadcasts to schools.
Crossword puzzle craze imported from America.
First flight to India and back, by Sir Alan Cobham.
General Election; Stanley Baldwin becomes PM (November).

1925   Locarno Pact – pledge of non-aggression by major European countries.
Charleston craze.
Ferguson light tractor in production.
National Playing Fields Association founded.
First flight to Cape Town and back, by Sir Alan Cobham.
First covered-top buses appear, in London.

1926   General Strike (3-12 May).
Hadow Report on Education stresses need for system of primary and secondary education.
Central Electricity Board formed.
Sir Alan Cobham make the first solo flight to Australia and back.
Council for the Preservation of Rural England formed.
First traffic lights appear in cities.
Birth of the future Queen Elizabeth II (April).

1927   BBC becomes a Corporation.
First automatic telephone exchange opened (Holborn).
First solo transatlantic flight made by Lindbergh (May).

1928   Discovery of penicillin by Alexander Fleming.
Women of 21+ get the vote.
Test Matches begin between England and the West Indies.
First Mickey Mouse cartoons.
The Bank of England issues £1 and 10s notes.
John Logie Baird transmits the first television pictures between London and New York.
"Talkies" arrive from America.
Kellog Pact – renunciation of war by several countries including Britain, America, France and Japan.

1929   General Election; Ramsay MacDonald PM with 2nd Labour Government (June).
Margaret Bondfield first woman Cabinet Member.
World Jamboree of Boy Scouts at Birkenhead.
Test flights of the airships R100 and R101.
Wall Street Crash in America: start of general world economic crisis (October).

1930   First solo flight to Australia by a woman, Amy Johnson.
R101 crashes in France (October).
Youth Hostel Association founded.
Women's League of Health and Beauty founded.
First British Empire Games held, at Ontario.
First experimental television play transmitted.

Glossary

armistice	end of fighting
Art Deco	name given to the decorative style of the 1920s and 1930s
Attorney General	chief legal officer of the Crown
bob	short hairstyle for a woman
Bolshevism	political philosophy of the Bolsheviks, the radical group of the Russian Social Democratic Party, which seized power in 1917
charabanc	open coach used for excursions
Charleston	popular dance imported from America
cloche	close-fitting hat worn by girls and women
copper	large copper tub which was used for boiling clothes or heating up water
Council houses	houses built by local authorities and subsidized by the Government
crystal set	early wireless set which used crystals to direct incoming air waves
Drill	PE
Eton crop	woman's hair-cut like a man's
Fair Isle	name given to brightly patterned jerseys
Fairy cycle	two-wheeler bicycle
Flapper	modern girl
hip-bath	portable metal bath with room to sit in but not to lie down
liberty bodice	warm winter vest worn by girls
mangle	machine with rollers, used to squeeze out water from washed clothes, etc
Marcel Wave	artificial wave put into the hair by curling tongs (like a perm)
owner-occupier	person who owns and lives in his house
Oxford Bags	trousers with very wide legs
pebble dash	wall surface made by spraying gravel into soft plaster, usually painted
Picture Palace	cinema
red-brick universities	universities founded in Victorian times, eg Manchester and Reading
ribbon development	continuous building along the edges of main roads
service, go into	go to work in a big house, as a cook or maid
skivvy	home help
spats	short gaiters which covered part of a shoe. Often had side buttons, or strap under the foot. Worn by men
subsidize	provide money for
suburbs	housing development on the edges of towns
suffrage	right to vote in elections
talkies	first talking films
trams	electrified buses that ran on lines in the middle of roads

Places to Visit

Many museums have artefacts relating to the 1920s, especially costume, toys and household objects. In particular, the following have either specific displays on the 1920s or a large collection of objects from this decade.

HOMES
Black Country Museum, Tipton Road, Dudley, West Midlands
Brewhouse Yard, Castle Boulevard, Nottingham
Castle Museum, York
First Garden City Museum, 296 Norton Way, Letchworth, Herts
Kircaldy Museums and Art Gallery, War Memorial Gardens, Kircaldy, Fife
Museum of London, London Wall
North of England Open Air Museum, Beamish, Stanley, County Durham
Science Museum, Exhibition Road, London
Museum of Science and Industry, Newhall Street, Birmingham

CLOTHES
Gallery of English Costume, Platt Fields, Manchester
Museum of Costume, Alfred Street, Bath
Victoria and Albert Museum, Cromwell Road, South Kensington
Wygston's House, Museum of Costume, Leicester

AMUSEMENTS
Bethnal Green Museum of Childhood, Cambridge Heath Road, London
Castle Museum, York
Museum of Childhood and Gillow Museum, Judges' Lodgings, Church Street, Lancaster
Museum of Childhood, Sudbury Hall, Derbyshire
National Wireless Museum, Isle of Wight
Pollock's Toys Museum, 1 Scala Street, London

TRANSPORT
Museum of Transport, Albert Drive, Glasgow
National Motor Museum, Beaulieu, Hants
National Museum of British Road Transport, Cook Street, Coventry
National Railway Museum, York
National Tramway Museum, Crich, Derbyshire
Shuttleworth Collection of Historic Aeroplanes, Cars and Bicycles, Old Warden, Beds

Books for Further Reading

For Teachers
Branson, Noreen, *Britain in the Nineteen Twenties* (Weidenfeld and Nicolson)
Burnell, J., *A Social History of Housing 1815-1970* (Methuen)
Jackson, Lionel, *Fit for Heroes, a scrapbook of Britain between the Wars* (Blackie)
Wood, Sydney, *Britain's Inter War Years* (Blackie)
Leslie Bailey's Scrapbooks, Vol 2 1918-1939 (BBC)

For Children
Briggs, Asa, *They Saw it Happen 1897-1940* (Basil Blackwell)
Ellacott, S.E., *A History of Everyday Things, Vol V 1914-68* (Batsford)
Kelsall, Freda, *How We Used to Live* (MacDonald Educational)
Metcalf, Jean, *Sunnylea, a 1920s' Childhood Remembered* (Michael Joseph)
Wilkins, Frances, *Growing Up Between the Wars* (Batsford)

Index